C000000897

IMAGES OF ENGLAND

Clay Cross &
The Clay Cross
Company

George Stephenson, the founder of the Clay Cross Company, standing on Chat Moss. He once remarked that 'the strength of Britain lies in her iron and coal beds.... The Lord Chancellor now sits upon a bag of wool; but wool has ceased to be emblematic of the staple commodity of England. He ought rather to sit on a bag of coal'. Although it was often recorded that the Clay Cross Company commenced in 1837, there is no documentary evidence to substantiate this and the company's records show that it was a one-man concern established in February 1838. It was not until January 1839, that any shareholders joined him in his Clay Cross venture. An advert for the sale of the prints of this portrait appeared in the *Derbyshire Courier*, 12th May 1849.

IMAGES OF ENGLAND

Clay Cross & The Clay Cross Company

Cliff Williams

NONSUCH

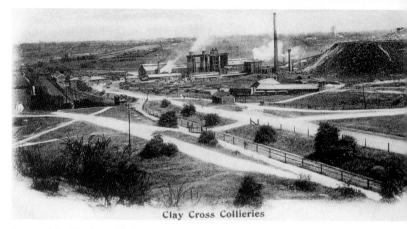

Clay Cross Collieries

A view of the Clay Cross Works, *c.* 1910, showing the furnaces and foundry in the centre with No.3 Pit waste tip and slag heaps to the right. This picture was taken off the No.1 coal and iron pit tip that extended well into Clay Cross and part of it can still be seen situated behind Kwik Save. Note the turrets of the castellated northern entrance to the left.

The author and publishers acknowledge the help and support provided by Biwater Pipes.

First published 1995
This new pocket edition 2005
Images unchanged from first edition

Nonsuch Publishing Limited
The Mill, Brimscombe Port,
Stroud, Gloucestershire, GL5 2QG
www.nonsuch-publishing.com

© Cliff Williams, 1995

British Library Cataloguing in Publication Data.
A catalogue record for this book is available from the British Library.

ISBN 1-84588-142-7

Typesetting and origination by Nonsuch Publishing Limited
Printed in Great Britain by Oaklands Book Services Limited

Contents

Acknowledgements

My sincere thanks must go to Alan Harris who has so generously given up his time and been so supportive throughout this project, carefully helping me to sift through the company's records and ephemera. Equally, my thanks go to the Biwater Company for giving me access to their archives at Clay Cross and allowing me to reproduce a number of photographs and documents that have enriched this book. Also thanks to Dick Childs who, before his retirement from the Biwater Company, gave me much advise and support which has helped with this and other research concerning the history of the Company. A big thanks to Nancy March who ensured my larynx was well lubricated with a good cup of char during my research session at the Company! Also, sincere thanks to the memory of the late Michael Richard Hale whose photographic expertise enhanced several old photographs used in this volume. Many thanks to Mr J.H. Price for contributions and help with the Crich and Ambergate Limeworks and to Mr D. Sparks for help with the Ashover Light Railway. Thanks to Dr David Edwards for information on the CXC's coke ovens.

Sincere thanks are also extended to the following who have in various ways contributed to this study, either by loaning a photograph or supplying information that has helped to remove some of the veneers and silences: Mr Jack Briddon, Mr Eric Briddon, Mr Sid Kilpin, Mr Walter Armstrong, Mr Geoff Smith, Mr Pete Large, Mr Ernie Frakes, Mr Basil Holocuk, Mrs Rene Pearson, Mr Wilf Hallowes, Mr William Deakin, Mr Stuart Band, Mr Peter Maskrey, Mr John 'Pomey' Turner, Mr Jimmy 'Utik' Cook, Mr Colin Bacon, Mr Alan Allsop, Mr John Robinson, Mr Dick Rees, Mr Joe Walton, Mrs Doreen Bowler, Paul Hooper, Mrs Anna Churms and the good company of the Salvation Army.

Special thanks to all the staff in the local studies section at the Chesterfield Library who have courteously and effectively dealt with all my queries and requests and to the North Wingfield History Group who have given their support and continued interest in this project.

Finally, many thanks to my wife Anne and my two daughters Anne-Marie Parker and Rachel for their patience and good humour during the time it has taken to complete this book and without whose cooperation it would not have been completed! If anyone who should have appeared here and has been omitted, I hope they will accept my apologies for their exclusion.

This Biwater Pipes 'sculpture' incorporating their 1994, Queen's Award to Industry depicting the new cupolas and pipe bank symbolises the continuity of over 150 years of iron production on the very same site commenced by George Stephenson in 1848. Biwater Pipes Limited are the current custodians of the Stephenson and Clay Cross Company archive from which much of the information for this publication has been researched.

Introduction

Invariably, the introductions to picture postcard and other old photograph books emphasise that these productions are not histories of the places they depict and this volume conforms to that tradition. So often, only a little is known about these images and many of them will retain their veneers and anonymity, despite the hours of research that has been done on them. Hopefully though, readers will be able help to remove some of the remaining anonymity by recognising some of the faces and thereby add to our knowledge and understanding of some of the images in this book.

Despite the book's limitations, it does reveal some evocative and valuable images. There are photographs that were previously hidden away in attics, biscuit tins, bottom drawers and also in the Biwater archives and together they make an important contribution to our understanding of the history of Clay Cross and the Clay Cross Company (CXC). Hopefully too, it contributes usefully to our knowledge of the industrial and social history of the County.

Clay Cross is a classic product of the Industrial Revolution. It grew from a small farming community into a dynamic and rumbustious industrial town dominated by the CXC. Its metamorphosis was commenced with the driving of the Clay

Cross Tunnel in 1837, and the simultaneous development of George Stephenson's collieries and coke ovens. In 1838 Stephenson set up a small company and in the following year, in order to attract capital, he invited his friends of the 'Liverpol Party' to invest in, and thus help establish, the 'George Stephenson Company', later to be renamed the Clay Cross Company, in 1851.

This pictorial volume is, therefore, predominantly about the CXC's industrial activity, depicting coalmining, coke ovens, limeworks, farming, foundry and furnaces, etc., that attracted much labour and caused a demographic explosion, increasing the population by 260% from 546 in 1831 to 1,478 in 1841. This book also projects the company's paternalistic investment in schools, housing, chapels and churches that helped to retain labour and cultivate a core of sobriety and subservience. Where buildings have been demolished and for which old photographs are not available, contemporary photographs have sometimes been used making the book a sort of visual directory of local industry and the town.

Because of time contraints and the elusiveness of some sources, there are gaps in the story that some will detect and no doubt there are 'mistakes' too that will be spotted. This project is not above constructive criticism! If there are any additions or corrections to be made please let me know about them. In many ways the book is already a community effort with many people helping and supporting it, by the donation of photographs or putting names to faces. No one has a monopoly in the pursuit of our town's history but I hope my efforts, like those of the late Frank Dwelly's, Dr Stanley Chapman's, Terry Judge's, Bob Gratton's, David Skinner's and Julie Langdon's, will go some way to making a contribution to the history of our town and one that will continue to inform and entertain its readers for many years and perhaps encourage others to take up the pen and explore the rich and fascinating historical resources at our diposal.

I would like to make an appeal to readers, also, for material and photographs that I feel sure must have survived somewhere. For example, one omission in section eleven is the absence of a picture of the Old Primitive Methodist Chapel, once situated on Bridge Street at the bottom of Eyre Street (Black Horse Street). There are also several picture 'gaps' in the Housing section and images of Bridge Street, Office Row and Smokey Green have eluded me and examples of these would be most welcome. If you have any of these I would be pleased to hear about them. A second volume is planned which would emphasise the role of the community, rather than the company, bringing together another collection of images like this, depicting streets, shops, pubs, football, cricket and people.

Hopefully, these pictorial histories will eventually be followed by a more comprehensive, economic and social history of the town, something that has long been awaited and, time permitting, will I hope also appear before too long.

The Nonsuch Publishing Company are to be congratulated on deciding to publish this book in their Pocket Images Series and I'm sure this issue will, because of its unique industrial content, appeal to a wider readership than Clay Cross. It will also give some context and background for family historians whose ancestors lived, worked and played in Clay Cross and provide a valuable resource for schools and colleges pursuing local history projects.

Collecting picture postcards is now an expensive hobby and several examples included in this book cost over £20 each – so the price of this book is a real 'snitch'! You can purchase here about 200 images for a fraction of the cost of a single postcard!

Cliff Williams

One

The Tunnel

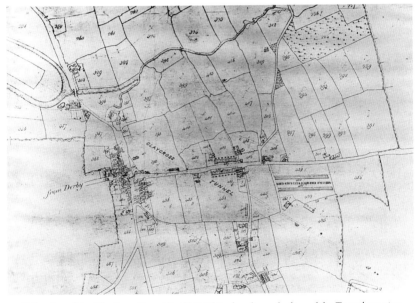

Tithe plan of the Clay Lane Township, 1841. This plan shows the line of the Tunnel running under the town and was mapped at the precise time of the town's metamorphosis that transformed it from an agrarian to an industrial economy. Top left shows the southern entrance and the Stretton spoil banks and the diversion of the Press Brook. The A61 running through the town followed the Roman Road, Rykneld Street which was turnpiked in 1756. Situated on either side of this road, near the centre, are the West and East Tunnel Rows built by the North Midland Railway Company in 1837 'for their superior workmen'. Just below this road, to the right, are the Top and Bottom Long Rows built by Stephenson in 1840. Situated below these, bottom right, are Stephenson's collieries and coke ovens.

The grand castellated, northern entrance to the Clay Cross Tunnel situated adjacent to the Clay Cross works. Excavations for the Tunnel commenced in February 1837, and the last brick of the arch was laid at the end of August 1839 and was the most difficult section of the seventy-two mile stretch from Derby to Leeds. The tunnel is just over a mile long and was driven directly under what later became the new town centre. George Stephenson and his son Robert were appointed Engineers-in-Chief of the N.M.R line at a joint salary of £2,000 per annum, plus travelling expenses.

Ventilation Shaft situated on High Street. This shaft was 144 feet deep standing almost in the centre of the tunnel and situated on the highest point of the N.M.R. at 360 feet above sea-level. The first sod was cut on this spot on 2nd February 1837, and about a year later the N.M.R. built the Tunnel Rows on either side of the A61 and close to this shaft.

Tunnel ventilation shaft situated in Market Street. During the first year of excavations four working shafts were sunk, with six more completed the following year, which enabled the tunnelling to proceed at twenty-two different places at the same time – inclusive of the two ends. At least fifteen excavators were killed during the time it took to complete the tunnel and many more were seriously injured.

The approach to the southern entrance at Stretton. A prodigious amount of soil, rock and clay had to be removed from the deep cuttings in order to reach the tunnel entrances. All this work was done by 'stout young men, round the waist of each is a strong belt, fastened to which is a rope running up the side of the cutting, and turning on a wheel at the top, whilst at the other extremity a horse is attached to the barrow being laden'.

A gang of plate-layers outside the tunnel entrance at Stretton, c. 1920. All the men are carrying naphtha oil flare lamps which issued a jet of flame for illumination. Note the long-handled hammer for knocking in the wooden keys holding the rails into the chairs attached to the base of the sleepers. Another man is equipped with a long spanner to tighten the nuts and bolts on the junction plates.

Fredrick Swanwick, resident engineer on the N.M.R. line, was born October 1810, in Chester and died in Chesterfield in November 1885. Swanwick bound himself apprentice to George Stephenson for four years and eight months from 5th October 1829, in the occupation of civil engineer. On the 23rd September 1836, he was appointed assistant engineer for the North Midland Railway and was 'resident engineer' for the seventy-two mile stretch from Derby to Leeds.

Smithy Moor Station at Stretton, *c.* 1900. This station was opened on the 11th April 1841, but its name was altered to Stretton for Ashover in 1872, when the Midland Raiway underwent a major restructuring. A new station building at Stretton was constructed in February 1889. The CXC decided to close their coal depot at this station in January 1933, and draw their supplies of coal from Clay Cross No.1 Wharf on Bridge Street and purchased a lorry for the delivery of coal in the district.

The North Midland Railway Inn, situated at the bottom of Highstairs Lane, Stretton was known as 'Bronco's' after John William Beighton, one of its landlords, who was frequently attired in a stetson. The landlord in 1889, was Mr Barton and the stationmaster was Mr Bradley.

Two

Proprietors and Gaffers

A portrait of George Hudson, 'Railway King', c. 1840. Hudson was one of Stephenson
and Co.'s original proprietors and together with George Stephenson, Robert Stephenson,
George Carr Glyn, Joseph Sanders, and Joshua Walmsley, made up the partnership in 1839.
Collectively, these people were known as the 'Liverpool Party' and all held two-twelfth equal
shares. Hudson sold his shares to Samuel Morton Peto in December 1851. William Jackson
was not one of the original shareholders and a did not aquire any shares until the company
diversified into iron production in 1847.

Samuel Morton Peto, c. 1839. He was one of the most influential and active shareholders and joined the company in June 1847, after acquiring one-twelfth share from George Carr Glyn. In 1851, he acquired the majority of shares, holding ten-twelfths and at this point the company changed its name to the Clay Cross Company (CXC). Peto laid the foundation stone of the company's school in August 1854.

John Walmsley MP had a close professional relationship with George Stephenson and accompanied him to Spain to examine the route of the Royal North of Spain Railway. In August 1847, the Company regaled about 700 workmen and their families with roast beef and plum pudding to celebrate five out of the seven proprietors, including Walmsley, being elected to Parliament. He relinquished his share to William Jackson in 1871.

Robert Stephenson, *c.* 1840. After the death of his father in 1848, he became the largest shareholder with four twelfth shares and was 'requested to accept the same position which his late lamented father occupied and that £500 per annum be placed at his credit for such general and professional duties'. In 1851, he severed his connections with the company when his railway interests conflicted with his company ones but he retained his interests in the Tapton Colliery until it closed in 1857.

George Carr Glyn, banker and later Lord Wolverton, was on the original directorate of the North Midland Railway Company and served as its chairman for a time. He was also chairman of the Railway Clearing House and of the North Western Railway but relinquished his shares to George Stephenson in June 1847.

William Jackson MP of Birkenhead was Chairman of the Company from 1862 to 1876 and acquired all the shares in December 1871. He entered Parliament in 1847, and represented Newcastle-under-Lyme until 1865. On the retirement of Mr Thornhill from his North Derbyshire seat he resigned Newcastle and was elected to represent that constituency. After the passing of the Reform Bill in 1867, North Derbyshire was split in to two parts and Jackson was defeated when he contested the new division. He married Elizabeth Hughes, the daughter of Lieutenant Hughes of Liverpool in 1829, and was created a baronet by Gladstone in 1869.

Charles Binns, general manager of the CXC from 1839 to 1881. This portrait was painted by Daniel Macknee RSA in 1869, and presented to him at Chesterfield by his friends in the district. He was born 23rd October 1813, the second son of Mr Jonathan Binns, land surveyor and estate agent of Lancaster. First educated at a private school in Lancaster and then at the Society of Friends School in Kendal after which he joined his father and qualified as a surveyor. In about 1832, he became private secretary to George Stephenson and was subsequently appointed agent to the Clay Cross Collieries in 1839. He was perhaps the most influential person in the town until his demise on the 12th January 1887, 'Being dead he will yet speak to the diligent to encourage them to fresh activity, to the idle to make them blush for their indolence, to the noble and generous to urge them to still nobler and more generous deeds, to the churlish to make them ashamed of their illiberality. A just and merciful magistrate, a warm and true hearted friend; a kind man and a concilliatory employer of labour, a liberal in politics tolerent of other mens' convictions, an easy master, faithful servant and benevolent man'. He was buried in Clay Cross Parish Churchyard together with the CXC's first generation of managers.

Thomas Hughes Jackson, chairman of the CXC from 1876 to 1930 and son of William Jackson jnr. He was educated at Harrow and entered the office of Messers T. and H. Littledale Company of Liverpool. After accompanying his father to Canada to construct the Western Railway he then completed a world tour. He became a member of the board of G. H. Fletcher, shipowners and brokers, and was also chairman of Queens Insurance Company. He was born in 1834, and married Hermine Meinertzhagen in 1853 and died in January 1930 and was buried in the family vault at Claybrick Hill Cemetery, Birkenhead. He was an absentee proprietor and resided at the Manor House Birkenhead.

The Gaffers, taken about 1870. Back row, from left top right, includes: Chas Bloor, underveiwer; Joseph Dickenson, general surface manager; George Kemp, draughtsman and William Hey, senior office worker. Front row, left to right: William Parker, underviewer; Thomas Wilkinson, cashier; William Howe, chief engineer and his son, George Howe, assistant engineer.

Managers and foremen outside Clay Cross Hall, c. 1920. It was usual for the company to wine and dine its officials about once a year. In May 1950, during a period of labour shortage and as an incentive to persuade employees to attend work regularly, the company decided to give a chicken at Christmas, to all those employees who maintained a full attendance record. One employee, Kenneth Baxter, told John Jackson MD that if he worked all year without a day off work he would want Coney Green Farm!

Left: William Howe, engineer was born 3 March 1814, at West Auckland in County Durham. He worked with his father as a colliery carpenter and millwright from twelve to twenty-one years of age. In 1836, he was employed as a pattern maker at the Vulcan Foundry, near Warrington and then moved to Hawks and Crawshaw Company at Gateshead. Soon afterwards he was employed by Robert Stephenson at his locomotive works in Newcastle.

Below: The Link Motion which was said to have been invented by William Howe whilst he was employed at Newcastle. There is much controversy about who actually invented this device as it was never patented, but at the time Howe was given twenty guineas and promoted to senior engineer at the Clay Cross Collieries, in 1846. In 1872, he was presented with a gold watch and a purse of £200 for having 'practically' developed the invention. He died at Clay Cross 16 January 1879, aged 65 years.

Three

Coke Ovens

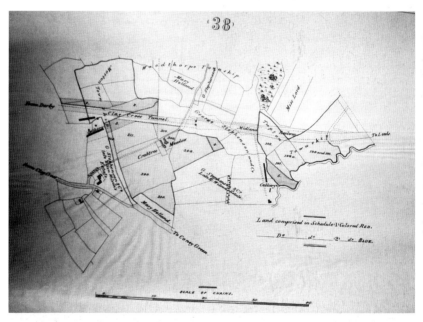

An early plan of Stephenson's coke ovens and collieries, c. 1840. The No.1 Pit sunk in 1838, and the first batch of experimental coke ovens built in 1839, are located on the old incline almost lying across the tunnel. Note the the castellated northern entrance marked on the plan and another batch of ovens near to the No.2 Pit, site close to the River Rother. Also see the Tupton Colliery incline and loop that connected up with the N.M.R line at Clay Cross Station. This colliery was sunk in 1840/41 by Chambers and Coke of the Wingerworth Colliery Company and was taken over by the CXC in 1853.

Mr Albert Heath's photograph of the old and new coke ovens. After experiments with coking the Blackshale coal in 1839, Stephenson built a batch of coke ovens at the top of the Clay Cross incline with the idea of selling coke to various railway companies to fire their locomotives. Until the late 1860s coke was practically the only fuel used for locomotives but a modification of the firebox in 1870, allowed the use of coal.

A batch of Bee-Hive coke ovens originally built in 1840. Soon after erecting his first set of ovens Stephenson recruited a few specialist coke workers to operate them and in 1841 the census reveals that thirteen coke burners resided in Clay Cross and eight of them came from outside the county. The obituary of John Cutts, Pilsley, February 1892, records him has having had the coke-burning contract with the CXC for many years.

CHESTERFIELD GAS AND WATER SHARES.—Wednesday the two shares in the Chesterfield Gas and Water Company, advertised in our paper last week, were bought in for 100 guineas each. Bona fide bids of £100 each were made. The original price per share was £25.

AFFRAY AT CLAY CROSS.—At a late hour on Saturday night last, the 20th instant, some of the coke-burners and some of the brick-makers quarreled and fought on the turnpike road at Clay Cross; and from what occurred, it may be considered very fortunate that the affair did not end more seriously. The coke-burners, it seems, not finding themselves a match for the other party, drew knives of a dangerous description, having large blades, with springs at the back to hold them open. In consequence, one of the brickmakers was cut across the arm and stabbed in several places in the side. His wounds, it is hoped, will not prove so dangerous as was at first apprehended.

CHAPEL-EN-LE-FRITH FAIR.—This fair was held on the 18th instant. There was a good show of cattle. Both calvers and barreners were on the decline, and few changed hands. Of pigs there was a good show, and many were sold at lower prices.

CHAPEL-EN-LE-FRITH.—The anniversary sermon in behalf of the Wesleyan Methodist Sunday School was preached in the Wesleyan Methodist chapel, by the Rev. Mr. Burton, from Sheffield. The rev. gentleman illus-

Simplex Coke Ovens, *c.* 1910. By the turn of the century the Beehive ovens were obsolete and in October 1903, the Simplex Coke Oven Company commenced erecting eight experimental ovens and completed them by March 1904. The old ovens were closed down in 1905 and by 1906 the company were operating fifty six new Simplex ovens. This system was invented by the Belgians and processed waste gases from coking to make tar and ammonia.

The Simplex Ovens looking north from the coal storage bunker. Continuing to improve their coking and by product capacity the company decided, in September 1923, to install some regenerative ovens. Initially the contract was with the Societe Anonym de Constructions but unfortunately they went bankrupt and reneged on the contract but paid the CXC £1,000 compensation.

A view from the 'ram side' of twenty of the original thirty-four waste-heat ovens and the sixteen newer ones at the further end. Although the replacement of these Simplex ovens for the Regenerative Type became the subject of litigation, the company borrowed £25,000 in February 1930, to complete the work. Some fifty five new ovens were completed in the following year which more than doubled the coking capacity, producing about 3,000 tons per week.

Personnel grouped on the ram side of the ovens near the coal storage bunker. The corrugated iron structure is the combined ram and coal compression machine. The three men standing to the right of the picture are George Howe (foot on rail), Otto Hahn, coke ovens manager (smoking pipe) and George Bramley. Albert Greatorex, 114 High Street, was foreman of the coke ovens from 1908, until his death in 1938.

The 'Cracker' plant for crushing the slag produced by the furnaces. In October, 1913, the company authorised expenditure of £1,200 for the erection of a Tar Macadam Plant that could deal with the production of 100 tons of material per day. A reference in the company's memo book 1878/79 refers to the making of 25,544 gallons of gas tar. The manager of the Slag department, for many years, was Reginald Slack of Thanet Street. He died in May 1936.

Clay Cross Brickworks, c. 1933. The company had been making bricks for its own use from about 1840. In 1896 they installed a Bradley and Craven brick making machine and four kilns capable of producing 1,000 common bricks per hour. In December 1916, £2,500 was spent on erecting a Patent Brick Kiln. These works appeared to close down about 1930, and, after reconditioning at a cost of £1,000, started up again in July 1933. They finally closed 28th January 1955.

Four

Furnaces, Pipe Pits and Spun

The Works from the west, 1958. This comprehensive shot overlooking the Midland Line depicts much of the company's industrial activities at Clay Cross which have been rooted in this area since its commencement in 1838. Central to the picture are the foundry, blast furnaces and spun with the No.2 pit chimney and pumping structure to the left. To the immediate right is the old furnace wall, power house and cooling towers, behind to the right is a massive slag heap and further right, two gasometers.

Furnaces, *c.* 1870. In October 1846, it was decided to build two furnaces at a cost of £24,000 to maximise the use of small coal that could be burnt into coke for the production of pig iron. During the time this work was proceeding Binns, general manager, was asked to write to the manager of the Sparrow Iron Works, Staffordshire, to ascertain the value of their coal and coke for the production of pig-iron. These furnaces were completed and blown in May 1848 and to celebrate the occasion a dinner was held in the New Inn, Market Street. About 1850, the Furnace Inn (now The Old English) was built and acquired its name from the company's new enterprise.

Opposite above: A rare view of the top of the furnaces, *c.* 1870, showing the furnace being charged with limestone. The full barrows were hauled up on the steam-driven lift and wheeled to the relevant furnace. The 1851 census return records eleven furnace workers, two furnace keepers and four moulders, with one apprentice, seven years of age.

Opposite below: In the early days before any specialisation and the building of their foundry the company were simply interested in producing pig-iron and the above photo shows the preparation of the pig-beds. Prior to the building of the furnaces the company were selling ironstone and reclaimed about 200 tons from the tunnel spoil heaps. The two main iron stone rakes in the vicinity were the Black and Brown Rakes. The spoil heaps are still visible behind Kwik Save.

Above: A front view of the furnaces, *c.* 1870. In 1848, the two furnaces were producing about 200 tons per week and when some technical improvements were made in 1850, production increased to 240 tons per week. A third furnace was built in 1854 and other improvements in 1870 increased production to 480 tons per week. Note the Clay Cross wagon to the left and the workers in the process of loading the barrows.

Left: In anticipation of the demand for more iron for their new spun plant, No.3 blast furnace building commenced in April 1936, at a cost of £6,000. It was ready for putting into blast in February 1938 but was not lighted until 20 July 1939, when Miss Ann Jackson, daughter of Lt. Col. H.H.Jackson, performed the lighting ceremony. James Langdale was the manager of the furnace department at this time.

Tapping of the new blast furnace in 1939. This furnace was the first since the original ones to be put on a new foundation. It was seventy-two feet in height and expected to produce 1,000 tons per week. By the 1950s, this plant was virtually obselete and the foundry somewhat antiquated. Closing the entire plant was considered. Work commenced on demolishing these old blast furnaces in 1959 and the new hot-blast furnaces came into full production on the 27 November 1961.

The large furnace wall running between the two large chimneys dominates this picture. The postmark on the back of this postcard is dated 30 June 1908, and reads, 'Just a line to say am alright. On nights this week. This is the iron works showing the furnaces. The church is at the back on the top of the hill. The single railway is the goods line to the Clay X town Goods Station. The main line to Derby Tunnel is directly underneath. So long, hope all well love W.'

This large foundry was commenced in 1864 and shows the 'All Nations' pipe pit looking down to the foundry end. Initially the company produced cast iron pipes, vertically cast, for gas, water and steam pipes. At one time there were eight pipe pits – Well's Pit, All Nations Pit, Joe Ghosts Pit, Charlie Tooley's Pit, Walter Taylor's Pit, Charlie Titterton's Pit, Tommy Whitworth's Pit ('marrionetts') and Jack Pearson's Pit.

No.5 Economiser Pit 1910. In November 1896, it was decided to install a new pipe pit to produce 5,000 economiser tubes for Messers Goodbrand and Company, Manchester with a further order to follow of 10,000. Delivery was made at fifty per day with a daily profit calculated at £1 17s 6d. In October 1919, the company were asked to be a partner with an Indian Pipe Foundry but declined the offer.

Please write us for prices of our celebrated House Coals, which we can deliver from our London Depots. Also Cast Iron Gas and Water Pipes of any size, strength and section. Special Brand C. + C. Pig Iron, and Best Derbyshire Picked Lime.

Chief London Office:—19, EASTCHEAP, E.C.

Bottom pipe bank showing flanged pipes in 1911. The CXC were one of the first company's to make use of postcards to advertise their products. This series of postcards comprised 25 views, 'Quite unique in character!' and for every complete set presented (but not neccessarily given up) by any of their customers, at the Company's Office, 71 Seymour Street, Edgeware Road the Clay Cross Co will make a FREE GIFT of one of four handsome pictures.

A contemporary view of Biwater's top pipe bank in 1995. The old furnace wall, an important structure of industrial history, can be seen on the left and the new hot-blast cupola built in 1990, is situated just a few yards from the original furnace site of 1847. At the time of writing the company have won a contract with the Indian Ocean island of Mauritius to supply about 27km of pipes and fittings.

The CXC's largest ever vertical cast pipe with a twenty seven inch diameter made in 1942. Roy Buckland is standing in front of the pipes and behind, from left to right are: Jack Briddon, Bernard Hobben, George Pearson, V. Whitworth, Frank Stanhope, R. Barker and J. Lawton. Mounted on top of the large pipe is a two inch pipe, the company's smallest. This large pipe was cast in the No.8 pit built in 1934, at a cost of £2,000.

CXC's letter head October 1917. The economiser was a simple apparatus to save fuel costs by employing waste heat from the flue gases to pre-heat the water fed to the boilers, an idea first used by a Wakefield firm in about 1845. To help with the sale of their products the CXC recruited David Rushworth who was making these units for Goodbrand and Co in Manchester. He built up a healthy market for their use in hospitals, workhouses and factories.

Benny Fletcher and workmate loading economisers onto an LMS waggon using a steam-crane. In November 1923, the CXC through A.R.Brown McFarlane, Glasgow, and their Japanese House, Yonei Shoken, Tokyo, won the sole agreement for the agency to sell fuel economisers to Japan and her colonies and dependencies. There is no evidence of any sales to Japan and in January 1933 it was reported that enquiries for the export of pipes are proceeding. The Company stopped making economisers about 1956.

A view of the top pipe bank, c. 1940. This shows the No.2 Pit headstocks, winding engine, boiler-house and chimney, to the right. Standing immediately behind is the No.2 pumping engine and the bridge over the Erewash Line to North Wingfield. In the distance, about centre, is the chimney of the No.4 Pit with its pit-tip emerging from the left and the buildings to the far left are the regenerative coke ovens.

Opposite above: Spun Plant 1937, showing a six-inch diameter pipe, eighteen feet in length being lifted from the mould. In June 1932, it was reported that a 'gentleman' wished to enter into the company's service with a view to manufacturing Spun Pipes. This gentleman, a Mr Jervis, had calculated that a plant with a capacity of producing sixty tons per day would cost about £13,000. The plant was completed in February 1935.

Opposite below: In 1938, the CXC was faced with a writ for the infringement of a patent relating to the use of silicon powder and its distribution in the manufacturing of spun pipes. In May 1941, the judge ruled that there had been an infringement of the patent by the CXC but the letters patent were invalid because there were no specifications about silicon content. The silicon tray and the ball that distributed the silicon through the pipe can be seen to the front-right of the picture.

A comprehensive south-eastern aeriel view of the CXC's works 1958.

Bottom pipe-bank with electric cranes in 1958, showing a gasometer structure to centre-left and and No.2 pit complex to the right and with the air-raid siren perched on the wooden pylon. This siren was first tested, together with another at their No.7 Pit, on Monday 21st August 1939. Special Constables reported on their 'effectiveness or otherwise of the warning'.

The old furnace wall with two of the company's wagons, now preserved for posterity, and the new hot blast cupola standing to the right. One of the company's biggest expenditures was the acquisition of railway wagons and, in 1846, they had purchased some 676 waggons valued at £43,012. In March 1884, they sold off 2,000 of them to the Midland Railway Company for £73,634.

Right: The Biwater Company, under the present management, are proud of their history and have designed and placed descriptive plaques on various surviving old buildings. They have also introduced a small museum on the premises which unfortunately has only limited access and should perhaps, one day, be housed elsewhere to give it the better access and publicity which it truly deserves.

Below: A view of the works from the the A61 about opposite the North East Derbyshire Snooker Centre, *c.* 1937. This postcard was sent to Miss Vera Reynolds, 24 Shellons Street, Folkstone and reads, 'X is the place where we work. There is a lot of girls work in the Foundry. Write and let me know if you want a job'.

The Works, Clay Cross

Eric Briddon at the wheel of his Maudsley A.E.C. engine, outside the CXC offices, ready to dispatch a consignment of pipes to Birkenhead Docks in 1949. This lorry was purchased second-hand in 1949, from Bernard Swain of Somercotes. In February 1952, the company ordered six Dennis diesel lorries for £20,000.

A seven ton, eighty four inch, special casting destined for the Liverpool Dry Docks and transported on a Pickford's low loader in 1974. From left to right, back row: Oswald Bainbridge, Charles Courtney, Jack Bradley, Bill Taylor and Bill Slainey (moulders), Frank Scoffins, Alan Walters, Les Williams, Alan Harris, John Orwin, Thomas Whitworth, Les Ball, Herbert Bradder. The person kneeling is Robert Tidman. Jack Briddon and Ernest Messenger tested this particular pipe.

Joe Herret working in the blacking-shed in 1958. This operation ground up coal dust and sand that was made into a paste and applied it to the mould to give the casting a quality finish.

Opposite: Ted Marshall stack moulding gland rings in the 'Big Shop' with Sid Jones tilting the ladle for casting. This foundry was built in 1865 for £544 and the following year it was extended at a further cost £744. The first iron moulders recorded in the employment of the Company in 1851, were George S. Grundy from Allsworth, Nottinghamshire. Living with him was his nephew Joseph Riley, aged seven years, who 'works at moulding'.

Bill Taylor and Tommy Whitworth ramming a special flange duckfoot bend with green sand in the 'Big Shop' in 1958. The 1861, census records thirty-five iron and foundry workers, increasing to fifty-nine in 1871, and seventy seven in 1881. The numbers continued to increase with the introduction of more pipe pits and economisers.

The old, but not original, pattern shop, built during the Great War and displaying Union Jack tiles on the roof. This business was moved to a new shop in 1992. The craftsmen shown on this photograph, from left to right, are: Fred Smith (patternmaker), Ken Matthews (apprentice patternmaker), Frank Scoffings (patternmaker) and Arthur Ralph (joiner). The last cast iron lamp-post made by the company, for Harrow Road London, can be seen on the right. The pattern was made by Oliver Holmes.

Five

Coney Green Farm

Coney Green Farm, c. 1883. In the picture, from left to right, are: Miss Bilby, Mrs Haynes, Mr Haynes (company baliff) and Miss Haynes. The farm, and most of the estate, was purchased by the CXC in 1873, from George Banks Wilson to make way for the extension of their works and to provide more tipping space for their furnace slag and refuse from No.2 and No.3 Pits. In April 1890, it was decided to pull it down and rebuild it on the opposite side of the road.

Left: An advertisement in the Derby Mercury for the sale of Coney Green Farm in November 1774. The Brailsford family, a very old North Wingfield family, were resident at Coney Green in the sixteenth century and in 1593, Elizabeth Brailsford was baptised in North Wingfileld Church 23 December, 1593.

Below: A plan of the farm and estate in 1842. The farm and gardens were well set out and show a large walled garden and the field, that incorporated two ponds, was referred to on the 1841, Tithe Plan, as Noah's Ark. A reference to 'Cunigreen' is recorded in the will of William Milnes of Henmill, Holmgate in October 1561, when he bequeathed 6/8d to the building of Cunnigree Bridge.

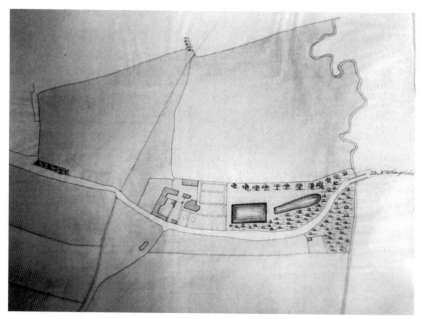

New Coney Green Farm, *c.* 1920. Between June 1890 and June 1892 some £2,000 was spent on rebuilding the farm and house using much of the same stone. Two of the old date stones, 1681 and 1810, were re-incorporated into the new buildings with the latter date bearing the initials 'TW', referring to Thomas Wilson who purchased the farm and estate for £4,000 in 1799. This family have a long lineage in the North Wingfield Parish and originate from Parkhouses.

CXC grade A milk supplied from the Coney Green Farm in 1910. At this date a bottling plant was introduced at a cost of £25. Prior to its introduction not more than ten gallons of the company's milk was reported to have been consumed daily in Clay Cross but shortly after its introduction it rose to thirty gallons. The retail milk round, together with two milk vans, were sold off in April 1951, for £2,300. The sale price was assessed on the daily sales figures of £8 to £9 per gallon.

Harvest-time in 1958. A view from the east showing Coney Green Farm. To the left, over the North Wingfield Road, is the Work's sports field and situated at the bottom of the field is the last remaining furnace ventilation shaft for the No.3 Pit. From as early as 1856, the company were producing gas for their works and the town. Two of the gasometers can be seen just right of centre.

'Gone are the days of the milkmaid. On at least one farm in Derbyshire the romantic maidens have ben displaced by the unromantic milking machine and the cows are mechanically milked. The milking is done by men, clad in white overalls and the scrupulous care which is taken in grooming the cows make it as near as can be, an impossibility for impurities to find their way into the milk'.

The *Clay Cross Chronicle* in April 1911, described the bottling department thus, 'It is first of all taken into the dairy, where it is strained into a large tank, all the milk being put together, thus ensuring a uniform quality. Then the new dairy outfit is put into requisition. The milk is strained into an automatic bottling machine, bottled in pints and half-pint bottles and sealed with a disc which has to be perforated before the milk can be obtained'.

Six

Crich and Ambergate Limeworks

An end view of the Ambergate limekilns, c. 1910. In 1840, George Stephenson decided to build a batch of twenty lime-kilns at Ambergate with the intention of making profitable use of the small coal and slack produced at Clay Cross, for the burning of limestone. This view shows the stationary steam lift at the end of the kilns that hauled up the coal to fire the kilns. It worked from 1841, until 1948, when it was replaced by electric haulage. In 1841, the company account books record an expenditure of £982 'to lime-works and stationary engine'.

A front view of the kilns, c. 1915, showing the addition of the cylindrical preheaters. By April 1840, twelve kilns had been erected at a cost of £5,106 and the following year another eight were added at a cost of £1,900 and the total cost of the railway and lime works at Chrich and Ambergate, including dead rents was £20,757.

A rear view of the same kilns showing the mineral railway spanning the Cromford Canal and tow-path. It was estimated that about 200 tons of limestone could be burnt each day and the highest tonnage burnt in any one year was 73.068 tons and this was achieved in 1937, and all cut and loaded by hand. It was also estimated that about six million tons passed through the kilns during the 124 years of production. They were closed in 1966.

The kilns at Ambergate were connected with the Chrich quarries by two self-acting inclines that covered a distance of some three miles and were described thus in April 1841, 'A short distance from Chrich the tramway passes through a tunnel between fifty and forty yards in length, cut through a rock composed of sandstone-grit. A little further on is an inclined plane which is worked by a wheel, round which passes a wire rope which lets down six wagons filled with limestone and draw up the same number of empty wagons. Nearly adjoining this is another inclined plane, which is uncommonly steep, rising at the rapid rate of one yard in three and half and is worked by a large drum, round which passes a wire rope; a lever is attached to the drum by which one man alone is able to regulate the speed of the wagon at pleasure, or stop them altogether. Two full wagons are let down and two empty ones are drawn up at the same time. The full wagons pass over the Cromford canal by a wooden bridge (elevated several feet above the surface of the water) to the top of the kilns'.

Hand boring a blasting hole in the Company's Chrich Quarry, c. 1900. In November 1840, Stephenson decided to subcontract out the work at Chrich Quarries for the baring, quarrying and breaking of limestone and for the burning, drawing and loading of lime. Production in the Chrich Quarry ceased on the 17th May 1957, and limestone was purchased from the neighbouring Deene Quarries.

Two loaded wagons at the head of the Steep about to be lowered, *c.* 1900. Note the large winding drum to the left that was installed by James Campbell, the CXC's first resident engineer who had previously worked for Stephenson at the Snibston Colliery. Campbell resided at Hill House, Clay Cross but moved on in 1846, and was replaced by William Howe.

A stunning view of the Steep, September 1952. This was a one in four steep and the kilns can be seen at the bottom. As the loaded wagons descend the incline their weight pulled the empty ones up. Historians tell us that this precarious incline was a favourite toy of Stephenson but for the workers it was a potential death trap and just after it opend a worker was thrown off a descending wagon and killed. In September 1842, Jerimiah Burton was killed when slowing down a wagon and a number of others have been incinerated in the kilns.

The original winding drum installed in 1840, worked continuously for nearly 120 years. This large wooden drum was mounted on baulks and revolved on a vertical axis with the wire rope guided to rise and fall on the drum as it wound and unwound. As the wagons careered down the slope they were checked by a hand-operated band brake. This brake was lined with wooden blocks and during dry spells they had to be damped with water to prevent them firing.

The limestone stockpile at the side of the Cromford Canal at Ambergate, c. 1900. This view shows the mineral railway bridge spanning the canal and tow-path. The canal was opened up in 1793 and large scale quarrying of limestone at Crich continued up to 1957. Since then the area has been transformed and is now the National Tramway Museum. Crich lime was also burnt in Stephenson's kilns at Loco Ford, Tapton, that were constructed in April 1842.

The Clay Cross Company's Grin Quarry at Burbage, Buxton, *c.* 1923. In December 1922, the company made an agreement with the Devonshire Estate to work their quarry and limeworks at Grin. A seperate limited liability company was set up in April 1923, with a capital of £20,000. The quarry and works were closed 30th June 1951 and the kilns finished drawing on the 23 June of that year.

Two of the Grin railway trucks about to be transported from Buxton to Ambergate 28 September 1951. Twenty-two of these eight ton spring buffer wagons were purchased from the Derbyshire Carriage and Wagon Company in 1933, for £9 10s each. The lorry is a Maudslay Mogel II, purchased new in 1950 for £3,000 from Oswald Tilletson's, Burnley. Standing to the left is Eric Briddon with his mate Arthur Heart. Alf Bowler (transport manager) took the photograph.

The 'Coffeepot' getting steam up in the Crich Quarry c.1900. The first steam locomotive introduced to these quarries was the No.6 engine, purchased from the N.M.R for £252 in 1841. This engine was primarily used for shunting coal up to the kiln lift. The 'Coffeepot', a vertical boilered 0-4-0 De Winton engine, was originally built in Caernarvon in 1875 and purchased by the Company in 1880. It was scrapped in 1924 and replaced by 'Tommy', brought over from Cranford in Northhamptonshire.

'Dowie' about to leave the weighbridge in Cliff Quarry with a train of limestone bound for Ambergate. This engine was purchased from Markham and Co Ltd of Chesterfield on the 10th February 1893, for £500. It was numbered No.38 on the CXC's engine list and was named after Mrs G.M.Jackson, whose nickname was Dowie. Note the Chrich Stand in the background which built in 1851 and was pulled down in 1922.

'Tommy', or 'William' as it was earlier called, was a twin model to 'Dowie' and was constructed by Oliver and Co Ltd of Chesterfield for the Cranford Ironstone Company in 1889, for £495. In 1924, the CXC decided to purchase 'William' and gave it a fleet number of No.37, it was then renamed 'Bridget' and in 1925, it became 'Tommy'.

Another picture of 'Dowie' equipped with new side saddle tank and dumb buffers added to all engines in the late 1930s. By the end of 1956, all the steam locos had been replaced by three diesels supplied by Rushton and Hornsby which continued in use in the quarry until 1957. One was used at the Ambergate kilns until their closure in 1965, and all three were sold in 1966.

'Hodder', was the last steam engine bought for the line at Chrich and was bult by Pecketts of Bristol in 1924, and acquired by the Clay Cross Company from William Twigg of Matlock. It first started working for the Fylde Water Board at Dale Head, near Clitheroe in Lancashire and then in the construction of the Stocks reservoir in the Hodder Valley, Yorkshire – hence its name.

From day one all the limestone in the quarries was got by hand. When considering a new lease in 1954, the company insisted on the option to break the lease on short notice and one of the reasons given was that 'our stone is got by hand we could not compete with the mechanically operated quarries'. In February 1957, it was reported that 'several of our employees will be retiring shortly in a few years and new 'blood' could not be attracted to a non mechanical limeworks'.

Seven

Ashover Light Railway

OPENING OF THE ASHOVER LIGHT RAILWAY.
April 6th 1925.

In December 1838, George Stephenson was considering the exploitation of the limestone deposits at Ashover and then again in February 1840. However, this scheme was not implemented by the CXC until 1925. Posing for this photograph in the Ashover School yard are, back row, from left to right: E.H. Ted Huddelston (quarry manager), John May (A.L.R. manager), Cap Guy Jackson (director), Colonel H.F. Stephens (A.L.R. engineer), Major H.H. Jackson (director). Front row, left to right: Henry A. Sandars (CXC solicitor), J. Steen (CXC secretary), T.H. Jackson (chairman), Gen G.M. Jackson (director) and R.O. Jackson (director).

The opening ceremony of the Ashover Light Railway, 6th April 1925. Two trains were provided for the occasion and the first to leave Clay Cross was 'Joan', followed by 'Peggy'. The driver of 'Joan' was Harry Revell and the fireman was Billy Towndrow but *en route* the four people standing to the left, Rachel Turbutt, Florence Jackson, Dorothy Johnson and T.H. Jackson, took their turn on the footplate.

All the A.L.R. steam locomotives were of the Baldwin type and named after General Jackson's three daughters and two surviving sons. This photograph shows 'Bridget' at Stretton in 1931. The three regular crew members standing, from left to right are: Bert Robinson (conductor), William 'Picker' Allen (fireman) and John William Banner (driver). 'Bridget' was named after General Jackson's youngest daughter, Elizabeth Bridget Huth Jackson and purchased from Thomas A. Ward in 1925.

'Peggy', near the Clay Cross and Egstow station steaming towards the Chesterfield embankment and Pirelli Bridge with driver Bill Banner. Named after General Jackson's eldest daughter, Margaret Beatrice Meinertzhagen Jackson who was nicknamed 'Peggy' – no wonder! The A.L.R. line was also known as the 'Peggy Line' by the locals.

'Joan', named after the second daughter of General Jackson, Hermina Joan Carmichael Jackson. She is seen here at Stretton Station in 1929 with conductor Bill Allen, about to close the crossing-gates. The A.L.R. ran parallel to the N.M.R. line from about the southern entrance of the Clay Cross Tunnel, up to the Ford Loop.

'Hummy', at Ashover during the summer of 1932. Named after General Jackson's second son, Henry Humphry Jackson. This locomotive was taken out of use in 1946 and eventualy cut up at Clay Cross in June 1951. He was joint MD from 1946 to 1969.

'Guy', named after Guy Rolf Jackson, the General's youngest son who became the joint MD in 1946 until his death in February 1966. His responsibilities were with the estates, farms and minerals. He was well-known as a cricketer and for nine seasons, 1922 to 1931, he captained the Derbyshire County cricket team and during the winter of 1927, he was given the captaincy of the M.C.C. team to tour South Africa.

The Pirelli bridge spanning the Chesterfield (A61) road showing 'Hummy' returning to the Clay Cross depot, about 1933. This plate girder bridge was installed in February 1923, and was a well-known landmark until demolished in 1951, leaving the western abutment and part of the embankment running towards the Hill Top loop.

Clay Cross and Egstow Station in 1928, where the day-to-day running of the railway was conducted under the management of Captain John May. The A.L.R. had six stations and seven halts on its seven mile route. It opened up for goods traffic in January 1924 and for daily passengers in April 1925, and the last public excursion train ran in June 1940.

Ashover (Butts) station 1926, with the United Methodist Free Church (Butts Chapel) visible to the right. The Butts was a favourite picnic spot for many Clay Cross people, particularly at Whistuntide and Easter. The main reason for the building of the A.L.R. was to take limestone to Clay Cross and most of this was got from the Butts Quarry.

Holmgate Halt looking down towards Clay Lane showing the 'last passenger' waiting for the 9.13 train to Clay Cross on Sunday 13th September 1936. Though the passenger service was suspended at this date the last public excursion train ran on the 8th June 1940, and the last special excursion ran on the 24th August 1947.

Eight

Clay Cross Collieries

Clay Cross No.2 Pit (second phase) commenced sinking in 1846 and was completed sometime in 1850. It was sunk on the old No.2 site close to the River Rother, to the west of Coney Green Bridge and in the township of Woodthorpe. It was closed in 1934, but continued to be used as an escape and pumping shaft for the No.7 Parkhouse Pit.

THE WINDING ENGINE DRIVER.
These men hold the lives of hundreds of miners in their hands every day, and haul to the surface thousands of tons of the celebrated "C.X.C. Gold Medal" Coal.

The No.2 Pit winding engine at Clay Cross with Mr Charles Housley at the controls. The Engineman's and Fireman's Association was established in 1892 and commenced with only forty seven members and its first general secratary was Samuel Rowarth of Clay Cross. The Wheeler, Housley, Marriott and Roworth families provided several generations of winders and firemen for the company. Joseph Wheeler was employed as a winder for 58 years at the No.4 Pit and he was succeeded by his son William in 1905.

No.3 Pit, situated to the left of the picture, was also on the Clay Cross Works and commenced sinking early in 1852, opening up for production in December 1853. It was eventually closed in 1910.

A 'holer' undercutting coal, ready to be dropped for loading into wagons. Note the dangerous position this collier has placed himself in, in front of the wooden props in an attempt to get a deeper cut. It was not until the 1900s, and the introduction of coal cutters, that machinery was used with any success to undercut coal. The miners' most important tools were the pick, shovel, hammer and wedge.

The caption for this CXC postcard may seem innocuous enough but a little investigation reveals a different story. When this photograph was posed for, in around 1910, it was, according to company rules, illegal to fill tubs with a shovel, and a fork was insisted upon. Before the company would concede to the use of a shovel they demanded that the men accept a reduction of 5d per ton in their basic rate.

The CXC did not send any exhibits to the Great Exhibition of 1851, but donated £9 1s in 'furtherance of the exhibition'. At the Franco-British Exhibition held in London in September 1908, the CXC was awarded two gold medals for their excellence in engineering work (economisers) and coalmining production. The Clay Cross Brotherhood Institute organised a trip for 295 people to visit the exhibition.

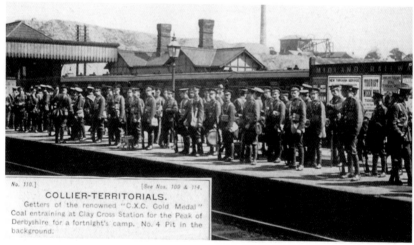

No. 110.]   [See Nos. 109 & 114.
COLLIER-TERRITORIALS.
Getters of the renowned "C.X.C. Gold Medal" Coal entraining at Clay Cross Station for the Peak of Derbyshire for a fortnight's camp. No. 4 Pit in the background.

No.4 Pit, sometimes refered to as the New Foundation or Ankerbold Colliery, commenced sinking about August 1854. Coal was reached in August 1857, and a celebratory dinner was held for the engineers and sinkers, in the Angel Inn, Clay Cross. This pit was situated behind the Clay Cross Station and its tandem headgear can be seen in the background. This was an expensive pit to sink requiring, ninety-six yards of tubbing and cost well over £20,000 to sink.

A young pony driver riding the 'limmers' and taking a train of 'full 'uns' to the No.2 Pit bottom, ready for the London market, the company's biggest customer. In 1844, the company had the distinction of being the first company in the country to send coal to London direct by rail.

No.5 and No.6 Pits, situated at Morton, c. 1910. No.5 Pit commenced sinking about June 1863 and by August 1865, the Blackshale Coal was reached at a depth of 300 yards. The No.6 Pit was sunk to the Hard Coal seam in June 1874 and cost about £18,000 to sink and about 100 men and officials celebrated the winning of the coal at the Station Hotel, Morton. These pits closed in 1964.

No. 105.]   **ON THE BELT.**
    One of the travelling tables (belts) along which the
    "C.X.C. Gold Medal" Coal is passed during its preparation
    for the London Market.

'Bat-scratchin'', removing the dirt from the coal at the Parkhouse No.7 Pit screens. This plate-belt was erected in 1895, at a cost of £700. The job was monotonous, dirty and back-breaking and amongst the lowest paid ones at the pit. At some pits it was the job of the old and injured. The person on the right is Tom Palfryman who worked for the company for sixty-four years, retiring at the age of 75.

The CXC's No.7 Parkhouse Pit commenced sinking in 1866 and was opened up to the Blackshale seam in May 1868. This event was celebrated at the Queens Head pub Clay Cross. The depth from the surface to the Blackshale Coal was 179 yards and the diameter of the downcast shaft thirteen feet and the upcast shaft was ten feet diameter and 100 yards deep. It cost about £18,000 to sink.

No. 124.   ARRIVAL AT DAYLIGHT.   [See No. 120.
Pony arriving at the top of the shaft after nearly 20
years in the bowels of the earth. Ponies not infrequently
spend nearly the whole of their lives underground. This
photo was taken at one of the Clay Cross Mines where the
celebrated "C.X.C. Gold Medal" Coal is produced.

This photograph shows gaffer George Dunn attired in a smoking-cap accompanied by the hostler, Mr Allsop, watching a pony being brought out of the pit. The Dunn family provided a host of deputies and officials for the CXC and were recruited in the Durham area from about the mid-1850s. In about 1910, the company had about 300 pit ponies.

The Parkhouse Pit tip in 1967, prior to opencast operations and looking towards the pig farm at Danesmoor, close to the Erewash Line. The gap running down to the right once accommodated the 'Blocks' that housed the pit's workforce. Gaffer Dunn lived down the pit lane at Copenhagen Farm, purchased for him in 1878 for £666.

No.9 and No.11 Pits, referred to as the Avenue Pits, were situated on the Wingerworth Estate. The No.9 Pit appears to have commenced sinking about January 1880, and the Blackshale was reached at a depth of 235 yards in March 1881. A No.10 Pit was contemplated but never sunk. No.11 Pit was actually sunk in 1850s by the Wingerworth Colliery company and purchased by the CXC in 1857. It was put into 'mothballs' until the 1880s.

The Clay Cross No.2 Pit man-rider that was powered by a direct steam driven rope. Note the electrician, Albert Wragg, equipped with rubber gloves and sporting a tie. He was the first apprentice electrician to be employed by the CXC. The company's first professional, electrical engineer recruited to introduce new and more sophisticated electrical apparatus to the works was Captain Raliegh Hills who came to Clay Cross in 1901. He died at Cromford in May 1937.

The Bonds Main Pit, situated at Temple Normanton, was sunk by the Staveley Company in 1898 and was named after George Bond the Staveley's senior colliery manager. It was purchased by the CXC in 1924, for about £21,600. At this pit the Blackshale had been worked out and the four seams left to work were the Tupton, Bottom Hard, Deep Soft and Ell Coal.

No. 106.] **PAY-DAY.**
Coal-getters entering Pay Office for their wages after a week's work getting the "C.X.C. Gold Medal" Coal. The weekly pay-bill totals some £5,000.

Pay-day for some of the underground workers from the CXC No.2 Pit, c. 1910. In August 1908, the CXC decided to alter the pay-day from Friday to Saturday – 'some wonder why, but the workmen and the employer knows, so do the trades people. He can get more money from the Saturday pay, for the people have not had their run on the money on Friday night. Then a headache does not keep the workmen at home on Saturday'.

An early account for the Clay Cross Collieries 25th October 1842. In October 1840, they had entered the London Market delivering coal partly by rail to Rugby and then onwards by canal. This account records thirty tons of Tupton coal being shipped in the Queen Victoria. In 1844, the Company sent 961 tons of coal to London by sea.

Nine

Disasters, Hospitals
and Sick Clubs

The remains of the the CXC No.2 Pit pumping engine and building. On the 11th July 1861, the CXC's No.2 Pit was flooded with an inundation of water from the No.1 Pit, drowning twenty-three men and boys. In May the following year, to ensure that this would not happen again, the company began sinking an exclusive pumping shaft some 130 yards deep. The new pumping engine was 300 H.P. with a cylinder of 84 ins diameter and with a 10ft stroke. The beam was constructed from wrought iron instead of cast iron following experience of the Hartley Colliery Disaster in 1862. Here the cast iron-beam broke and fell down the shaft, taking the brattice with it and blocking the ventilation and leading to the deaths of 204 men and boys.

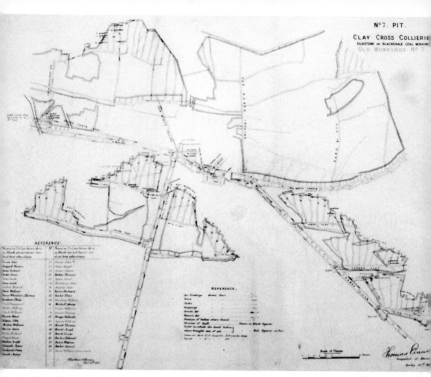

Nº 7. PIT.

CLAY CROSS COLLIERIE
SILKSTONE or BLACKSHALE COAL WORKING
OLD WORKINGS Nº 7.

At about 10am on 7th November, 1882, there was a firedamp explosion at the Parkhouse No.7 Pit which killed forty-five men and boys and this plan of the workings showing where the bodies were found by the rescue teams was submitted to the inquest hearing held first at the Queens Head pub and later at the Victoria Hotel. No miners were included on the jury which was instead dominated by local tradesmen.

The Parkhouse Pit memorial erected in 1884, in memory of the forty five men and boys killed. The unveiling ceremony was performed by Thomas Stendal Bryan an old collier and all the company's pits remained 'idle' for the day, at the request of the men. It was designed and furnished by Mr Rollinson, Chesterfield architect, stonework was by E. Tinkler of Clay Cross and the figure was carved by John Holden, carver and sculptor, from Broomhill, Sheffield. The cost was £160.

The Cemetery Entrance, Clay Cross

Valentines Series

North East Derbyshire District Council's tribute to Derbyshire miners past and present proudly dominates the High Street on the site where George Stephenson built Pleasant Row and adjacent to the ventilation shaft that was, until recently, enclosed in Pursgloves backyard.

Clay Cross Hall
nr Chesterfield. Novr 7. 82

My Dear Mr Jackson

When taking a walk round my garden this morning about ten I — heard a tremendous noise as if fifty cannon were firing off & looking round saw a great volume of — smoke issuing from your No 7 Pit. I had no doubt there had been a great explosion of fire damp & sent my Coachman — off at once to ascertain the cause & it was so Happily it was a — holiday & not many — men had gone to work.

The first page of a letter from Charles Binns to John Jackson relating how he heard the explosion at the Parkhouse Pit when taking a walk in his garden. The second page commences, 'Our men have gone down the upcast pit and are exploring and have brought some men out alive but it is greatly feared that some are dead. The afterdamp is very bad and some of the explorers have been overcome with it but none killed. I fear the pit shafts are much injured and the cost of repairs will be heavy but there is no present appearance of the pit having taken fire – John is over the moors but he's been sent for and if you would like to come I shall be very glad to give you a bed, etc. I am Dr [dear] Mr Jackson, sincerely yours, Chas Binns.'

Clay Cross No.1 rescue team, *c.* 1911. The Derbyshire and Nottinghamshire Coal Owners Association established a miners' rescue station at Mansfield Woodhouse in 1910, and the CXC contributed £1 per 500 tons for a first charge and £1 every 20,000 for the maintenance. The uniformed superintendant was ex-Sgt Major Huskinson who was in charge from 1910 to 1929.

The Derbyshire Miners' Convalescent Home at Skegness was opened on the 10th March 1928, by Lord Chelmsford. It was erected at a cost of £110,000, of which £50,000 was set aside from an endowment and the rest of the money was provided out of the miners' welfare fund from a levy of one pence per ton of output of coal in the county. It had accommodation for 150 patients, 120 men and 30 women.

The Order of Industrial Heroism was awarded to Joseph Shelton of Danesmoor on the 27 June 1925, for rescuing injured comrades that had been buried by a fall of coal on the face at the No.7 Pit. This award was inaugurated by the *Daily Herald*.

CXC's colliery hospital was built in October 1864, at a cost of £1,200. Prior to this the company rented the end-terraced house in Stoppard's Row as a hospital. The 1861 census returns record a family of three residing there with one patient hospitalised and the wife of the household was also the nurse. Sergeant Thomas Noton was the resident dispenser at the hospital from 1878 until about 1889 and doubled up as a sick visitor.

Nottingham Ancient Imperial United Order of Odd Fellows.

New Member's Admission Declaration.

Miners Pride Lodge,

held at The Midland Hotel

Every person desirous of being admitted a Member of the above Lodge, must pay a deposit of One Shilling before he can be proposed, which will be deducted from his Entrance Fee; if not admitted, it will be returned. He must also make the subjoined declaration :—

"*I hereby declare that* I am not at this time afflicted with or subject to any disease of an immediate tendency to shorten the duration of life; that I am not subject to any kind of fits, gout, rheumatism, or other Hereditary or periodical disorder; that I have no defect or disease in either of my eyes; nor am I troubled with any external or internal complaint that may in any way operate to my disadvantage, or incapacitate me from performing the usual duties of my trade or occupation; but on the contrary, that I am, to the best of my knowledge, a sound and healthy person; and that my age does not exceed **16** years."

(Signed) *George William Allibone*

Witness *Jas Whitworth* Date of Initiation *Nov 24* 19**00**

* In case a candidate is married, add the following after the word "that"—"neither myself nor my wife are" instead of the words "I am not." If not married, this Declaration must be signed again, should the Brother get married.

EACH CANDIDATE IS REQUESTED TO FILL UP THE FOLLOWING FORM.

Candidate's Name at full length *George William Allibone*

Candidate's Date of Birth *June 1st 1883*

Wife's Christian Name and Date of Birth

Place and Date of Marriage

Trade *Collier*

Residence *Hepthorne Lane*
North Wingfield
Chesterfield

NOTE.—Any person entering the above Lodge with a concealed infirmity upon him, will, if discovered, be excluded, and forfeit all monies he may have paid; and if any dispute shall arise concerning the age of a Member, before he can receive any benefit from the funds he must produce a copy of his baptismal register, or such other proof as may satisfy the Lodge. No person can be admitted a Member of the Nottingham Imperial Order (except honorary) after he has attained the age of FIFTY-FIVE YEARS.

THIS CERTIFICATE MUST BE CAREFULLY PRESERVED BY THE LODGE.

PRINTED BY P.G.M. JOHN HOWITT & SON, NOTTINGHAM.

The Miners' Pride Lodge Friendly Society was established in 1865 at Tupton and had its first HQ at the New Inn and then at the Midland Hotel at Hepthorn Lane, North Wingfield. This enrolment cerificate is for George Alibone, of Hepthorne Lane, a collier at the CXC's No.2 Pit. A good number of the enrolment and minute books for this lodge have survived together with several for the Sir William Jackson Lodge, established at Morton in 1870.

A TYPICAL CLAY CROSS COLLIER.
A getter of the "C.X.C. Gold Medal" Coal.

George Alibone of North Wingfield, *c.* 1910, proudly poses with his Bury's Pick and safety lamp, attired in his moleskins. Coal cutters, or the 'Iron Men' as they were frequently called, were not introduced to the CXC's pits until 1899 – 'Approved purchase of coal cutters for No.9 and No.5 Pits – estimated expenditure £850'. By 1900 there were only fifty-eight coal cutters being used in the county.

FEMALE
DEATH & DIVIDING SOCIETY

HELD AT THE

George & Dragon, Clay Cross

RULES.

1.—The Club shall be held on ~~FRIDAYS~~ *Tuesday* fortnightly, from 7 to 8-30 p.m. Entrance Fee **1**/- per member. Contribution **1/1** each Club night.

2.—Any person wishing to become a member must first give in their name to the Secretary, and shall be in benefit after six contributions have been paid.

3.—The age for joining is 16 years and not over 58 years.

4.—Any member being three contributions in arrears, and the same is not paid on the fourth night, shall be out of benefit.

5.—If the contributions paid to this Society are not sufficient to meet its demands, each member shall pay an equal levy, for that purpose.

6.—Each Member must show in each Quarter Night or will be fined **3d.**

7.—Any Member having a Claim on the Funds of this Society, must apply to the Secretary for a Note for the amount due for each Claim.

8.—On the last Club Night in the financial year, all Members must pay to the Society all contributions or other amounts due, according to the rules thereof. Any member failing to comply with this rule shall have no claim upon the surplus cash to be divided among the members.

9.—**The Benefits of this Society shall be as follows : Still-born, 5/- ; up to six months, 25/- ; over six months and under six years, £2 10s. ; over 6 years and under 12 years, £3 10s. ; over 12 years and as long as a child remains single, £5. No benefits will be paid under this or other rules unless such member is in benefit according to the rules of this Society.**

10.—If a member's husband die, she shall receive **£5** from this Society, or if a member die, the husband or other person having charge and management of the funeral shall receive **£5** providing the provisions of the previous rules have been complied with.

'Death and Divide' clubs played an important role in many Derbyshire mining communities and helped to avoid the stigma of a pauper's burial. These were initiated by the women who did not trust the company's sick and accident clubs and the central control of friendly society funds. Some clubs divided at Whitsuntide, Wakes Week or Christmas and one of these clubs is still running at the Midland Hotel at North Wingfield.

Many miners resisted the introduction of pit head baths and used all sorts of excuses such as immodesty of communal bathing, catching colds and weakening their backs, for not using them. However, the payment of 2d per week for the privilege was probably the main reason. The Coal Mines Act 1911, laid down that if a majority of two-thirds of the men required pit head baths the proprietors were requred to provide these facilities.

The CXC's Morton Colliery pithead baths opened July 1936. The opening ceremony was performed by Brig. General G.M.Jackson and G.F.Gardner, manager of the colliery, presided over the ceremony, with a large D.M.A contingent present. The finance for the scheme was provided by the Miners' Welfare Committee and cost about £14,000. The architect was A.J. Saise and provided bathing accomodation for 800 men with 68 bath cubicles.

Ten

Unions, Strikes and Lock Outs

Coal-picking on the No.1 Pit tip at Clay Cross during the 1893, Great Lock Out. On the 30th June 1893, the Federated Coalowners requested a 25% reduction in rate of wages and when the Miners Federation refused to concede, 300,000 miners were locked out until the 17th November. During the dispute, the Clay Cross Relief Committee distributed 45,000 meals together with £19 for groceries, £17 for fish and £125 for bread.

James Haslam, born in Clay Cross in 1842. He recieved a rudimentary education at the CXC's Stable School. He was a Primitive Methodist in adult life and became secretary of the Clay Cross Lodge of the South Yorkshire Miners' Association in 1875. He advocated the necessity for an independant county union and also became its secretary in 1880. In 1910 he was elected Member of Parliament for the Chesterfield Division, beating the Tory candidate by 1,664 votes.

A Derbyshire Miners' Union cap badge. In June 1889 6,000 of these were purchased and sold to members at a penny each. In May 1891, it was recorded that 'All members are desired to wear medals as the surest way to detect those unprincipled men who profess to be in the union, here or there, but in reality are nowhere. We have a lot of these men about and this is one way to detect them'.

A group of Pilsley miners proudly wearing their D.M.A cap badges at the Hard Coal Pit in 1895. The proprietors of this pit were typical union bashers and vigorously opposed the formation of the union at their pits but bowed to the inevitable when the union members struck work until every other man had joined the union. Houldsworth, one of the proprietors of the Pilsley Pit, resided at Alma House Clay Cross and sunk several pits both at Clay Cross and Pilsley.

Parkhouse No.7 Pit showing ponies being withdrawn during the 1893 lock out. Clearly the employers had anticipated and prepared for a long dispute and it was cheaper to put the ponies and horses out to grass. Pit ponies were usually incarcerated for life during the nineteenth century. In 1929 the CXC were fined £20 for allowing horses to be worked in unfit conditions and five ostlers were also fined £3 each, with costs.

The Danesmoor Lodge banner of the Derbyshire Miners' Union being paraded in the Market Square Chesterfield, *c.* 1890. The first miners' annual demonstration was held in Chesterfield in 1873, which attracted 30,000 visitors and was organsied by the South Yorkshire Miners' Association. The D.M.A held its own demonstration at Chesterfield in 1889, wich attracted fifty one lodges, accompanied by fifteen brass bands.

Opposite above: Outcropping during the 1926, General Strike in Houldsworth's fields, now, since 1934, the Kennings Park. The coal bassets out here, close to the Press Brook, and coal was mined here from at least the mid-sixteenth century. This was also the site for the Clay Cross Alma Colliery, sunk in 1854, and was also the name given to Houldsworth's colliery at North Wingfield, sunk in 1874.

Opposite below: Clay Cross Labour Party Womens' section 1926. This section was established after the 1921 dispute. They were an incredible tower of strength, supporting their husbands throughout, as they had done during the long diputes of the nineteenth century, particularly the 1866, Free Labour dispute and during the 1893 Great Lockout.

Branigan's Jazz Band at Clay Cross during the 1926 strike. Poverty was experienced during these long and bitter disputes in the inter-war years and this particular dispute caused severe hardship in every mining community in the county. To raise funds for soup kitchens a variety of activities were organised, including comic football and cricket matches and touring bands like this one.

Eleven

Schools, Chapels and Churches

Deer Leap Charity School was established 25th March 1790, by John Mottershaw. The schoolmaster lived here rent free and was paid 10/6d yearly for each scholar from the rent charge. No less than twenty-five scholars and no more than thirty were to be taught there. The yearly rent charge was paid by the owner of the farm and the £450 purchase money for the school was raised by Thomas Millward, John Brocksopp, William Webster, Jerimiah Higginbotham, John Mottershaw, James Millward and Edward Towndrow. Thomas Stanley was the schoolmaster there from 1790 until it closed in 1853.

The CXC's school was built in 1854 to teach the next generation of workers their 'relative duties in life'. The first schoolmaster was John Simmons who died suddenly in August 1856, at the age of twenty two years. He was replaced by Mr Hedgelong who emigrated to Australia in 1862 and he in turn was replaced by Joseph Stollard who did not retire until 1892. In the following year the schools were sold to the Clay Lane School Board for £5,500 and Mr Clark took over.

Following the introduction of the School Boards (Foster's Act 1870), those children whose father worked for the CXC but did not attend one of the Company's schools could attend a Board School. However, they had to pay for it and brass checks representing the amount of school fees were introduced. These were issued to the children and were accepted as payment at the various Board Schools. Kerslake, the Chesterfield Board School secretary, considered that, without school checks, the school pence would have been spent on beer.

The laying of the foundation stone at the first school built by the Clay Lane District Board School, erected 10th May 1894 (junior school). Standing, far left and at the front: J. Hoades, immediately behind him, with parchment: 'DC' reporter, behind him: the 'DT' reporter, to his right: J.S.May, Alfreton reporter, J.B.Fletcher, J.Stollard, J H.Unwin, G. Mycroft, J.Clark (sitting), W.B.M.Jackson; W.J.Drabble, A.Milner, J.Haslam, G.Redfern and, sitting on floor, Mr Rollinson, architect.

In 1853 the rent charge of the Deer Leap School was sold and the proceeds were used to build the Parochial Schools, at a cost of £400. This school was taught on sectarian principles laid down by the National Society for Promoting the Education of the Poor. Charles Binns and Joseph Oldham, the Clay Cross vicar, vigorously disagreed over educational policy and the CXC refused to give them a grant to build their school.

Danesmoor Bethel Chapel, New Connexion Methodist. The foundation stone was laid by Abraham Linacre and the chapel was opened 11th July 1869. The CXC donated the land and gave £50 towards the building fund. The company also rented the Chapel as an infant school in November 1869. Mr W.C.Hays of Clay Cross was the builder. The corrugated building immediately behind the chapel was the Sunday schoolroom erected in March 1907 and purchased for £30.

Bethel Chapel organ loft, installed 1907, when the chapel was renovated and a vestry added at a cost of £450. The CXC continued to lease this chapel for a school until Clay Lane District Board School built their new infants school at the top of the hill in December 1894 which opened up for pupils in January 1895.

Danesmoor Ebenezer Chapel, Primitive Methodist, also opened in July 1869. In May 1866, Danesmoor was missioned by the Primitive Methodists and succeeded in establishing a society of fifteen members and raising a 'Sabbath School of about seventy scholars who were instructed every Lords Day in a damp wash-house'.

The foundation stone for the St. Barnabus Church, at Danesmoor, was laid on the Wednesday 11th July 1883, by John Jackson JP, of the CXC, who was presented with a silver trowel to mark the occasion. Messers Rollinson and Son of Chesterfield were the architects but the belfry was not added until 1887. John Peter Jackson succeeded Charles Binns as general manager in October 1881 and resided at Stubbing Edge Hall, Ashover.

Clay Cross Town Band, choir, congregation and Danesmoor residents, posing outside the St Barnabus Church, 1909. The Church Room, situated behind the church, was opened by General Jackson in December 1908 – 'The building is of wood and iron erection built on brick foundations and is to be used as a church room for social and parochial gatherings and also as an institute for young men. A billiard table has been ordered'.

The old Wesleyan Chapel situated at the top of Holmgate. The foundation stone for this Chapel was laid 13th December 1847, by Charles Binns. It was closed in 1899 and purchased by R. Jones in 1900 who converted it into a dwelling and shop. A new foundation stone was laid on the 4th July 1900 and it was renamed Alma Lodge. In 1910 it became the Alma Printing Works which produced the *Clay Cross Chronicle*.

The Baptist Society in Clay Cross was established in 1864 and its meetings were held in a room adjoining a public house. In 1867 the Chapel was built in Market Street on a piece of land given by the CXC and the opening service was held in February 1868. The estimated cost of the building was £500, of which they collected £119, borrowed £100 from the Chapel Building Fund in London and friends in the neighbourhood lent £90.

This Baptist Church organ was installed in January 1908, and the opening ceremony was performed on 5th February by Mr Culverstone of Morton. The organ was a manual compass CC to A58 notes; CCC to F 30 notes, with pedals of the latest pattern to be adopted by the Royal College of Organists. The organ was built by Mr C. Loyd of Nottingham.

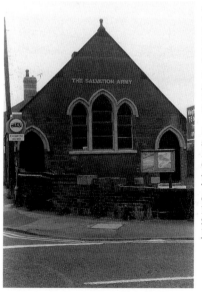

Above: The Baptist Sunday School Room was built in December 1879 and held its first service in January 1880. The site was purchased from the CXC and the plans prepared by W. Bramham. The building contract let to E. Tinkler for £560. The total cost of the building, inclusive of the heating (Timirills Patent Heating Apparatus), was about £700. It was sold to the Local Board of Health in 1893 for a sum of £900 to clear their debts on the building.

Left: The New Connexion Gospel Mission Hall situated in Thanet Street was formally opened 5th February 1902. The architect was Ernest Oxley and the builder was Eustace Tinkler who contracted to build the Mission for £641. The foundation stone of the first Peoples Gospel Hall was laid on 24 August 1874 by Mr Thomas Summerside of Ambergate. The Salvation Army has been incumbent here since June 1965.

The Free Methodist Church, Market Street, opened September 1888. This building cost about £2,000, inclusive of the site. The building was arranged with a large school hall on the lower floor with a rostrum at one end and class-rooms on the same level. The chapel could seat 350 people. The architects were Messers C.O. Ellison and Son of Liverpool and the builder, Eustace Tinkler. The Pentecostal Church purchased this building in December 1969, for £1,000.

Thanet Street showing the Catholic Chapel 'solemnly' opened for Divine service, 1st June 1862, by the Right Rev. De Roskell, Lord Bishop of Nottingham. The musical arrangements were made by Robert Durrance who presided at the harmonium. The chapel contains about two hundred sittings and was built in a neat, plain structure in the Gothic style with an 'open roof' and built of pressed bricks with stone dressings.

Above: Clay Cross, St.Bartholomew, *c.* 1913. The foundation stone was laid by Gladwin Turbutt on the 14th August 1849 and was consecrated on the 25th January 1851 by the Lord Bishop of Lichfield. 'With its increasing temporal advantage, the spiritual wants of its population, now numbering 2,500 souls, have not of neccesity, been administered to in any adequate degree, for the parish church of Northwingfield, besides being too far distant, is not sufficiently commodious to accommodate such a vast influx of inhabitants.'

Left: Builders repairing the spire and weather vein, *c.* 1915. The broach spire was added to the tower in 1857, built by Samuel Watts for about £370. The 'Cock' was mounted on the spire by William Howe, CXC engineer, as part of the Crimean Victory celebrations.

Right: Joseph Oldham was incumbent at Clay Cross from 1851 to 1888, after which he moved to the living of North Wingfield and was replaced by his nephew, the Reverend H. Oldham. The CXC minutes in September 1852, record, 'That £50 per annum be added to the stipend of the Reverend Oldham, incumbent at Clay Cross during the pleasure of the Company'. The majority of the CXC senior and middle management were Church of England.

Below: Inside the Church, *c.* 1910. This postcard was published by John Saunderson, hairdresser and stationer, of the Victoria Buildings, High Street who had been in business in Clay Cross from as early as 1851. The church was built on part of Gill Hill Close and given to the Church by the CXC, whose managers' tombstones dominate the west end of the graveyard and whose influence is also reflected in the stained glass and plaques inside the church.

Clay Cross New Connexion Chapel, c. 1920. The Connexion had a chapel on this site in 1824 but with the increasing population they built the above chapel in 1848 and this was replaced by the present chapel in 1972. This chapel had its own burial ground and a good many of the old gravestones can still be seen at the rear of the chapel.

Children from Clay Cross New Connexion Methodist, c. 1915, about to join the Whitwalk. All the children are in their 'Sunday Best', competing in the procession with a Band of Hope theme. The 'Death and Divide' clubs shared their money surplus at Whitsuntide which helped to buy new cloths for the Walk. At one time the Company gave prizes during August for the best dressed and cleanest children. Chapel Row is situated to the left and the Chapel is to the right.

New Connexion Sunday School, built 1869. In 1874 the CXC was threatened with the loss of government grants if it did not reduce the school population or increase school accommodation. They responded by renting this building for the infant classes in 1875 which was eventually given up to the Clay Lane School Board in 1892.

The Primitive Methodist Schoolroom situated at the end of Bridge Street and Market Street junction. Built in 1874, and extended in March 1910, at a cost of £800. The chapel and schoolroom were given up in 1935, when they amalgamated with the United Methodists. The trustees sublet the schoolrooms to Clay Cross Social Services in 1935 but a condition was imposed by the Company that the premises could not be used for political purposes.

METHODIST NEW CONNEXION,
CLAY CROSS.

70th SUNDAY SCHOOL ANNIVERSARY.

ON SUNDAY, MAY 6th, 1894,

THREE SERMONS

WILL BE PREACHED

In the Morning at 10.45, and in the Evening at 6 o'clock,

BY THE

REV. J. FOSTER

OF SHEFFIELD.

At Half-past Two in the Afternoon, by

G. WARRIS, ESQ.,

OF SHEFFIELD.

Hymns and Anthems will be sung by the Children and Choir.

On Monday, May 7th,

A PUBLIC TEA

Will be provided in the Schoolroom, at 5 o'clock; Tickets 9d. each. After Tea, a

⚜ PUBLIC MEETING ⚜

Will be held, to be addressed by the Rev. R. T. Rowley, Messrs. W. Smith, and G. Wharton, Dialogues and Recitations by the Children.

Chair to be taken at 7 o'clock, by Mr. G. MILLWARD,
Superintendent.

COLLECTIONS AT THE CLOSE OF EACH SERVICE.

H. WILDE, PRINTER, CLAY CROSS.

Methodist New Connexion Sunday School Anniversary 1894.

CLAY CROSS
❖ SUNDAY SCHOOL UNION. ❖

ARRANGEMENTS FOR THE

Whitsuntide Festival,

On Tuesday June 3rd,1884.

Place of Meeting:- PUBLIC HALL YARD.

All Schools and Bands to be on the Ground at 9.45 a.m. Singing to commence at 10 a.m. to be conducted by Mr. G. Millward.

PROGRAMME.

Hymn I. Raise the song of triumph!
Hymn II. The morning hours are few & fleet,
Hymn III Beautiful river,
Hymn IV. Press, on &c.

The Clay Cross Brass Band will play on each occasion of Singing.

Hymn Sheets & Tune Books will be sold, also, a Collection will be made on the ground.   (Collection after the 2nd Hymn.)

THE PROCESSION

will be Headed by the

CLAY CROSS BRASS BAND,

under the Leadership of Mr. W. Sears.   Route as usual.

The DRUM & FIFE BAND

will Head the Wesleyan School in Procession.

DANESMOOR BAND

will Head the Danesmoor School in Procession.

The Bands will play on the High Flat from 5 till 8 o'clock.

President:—	Treas:—	Sec:—
G. Silkstone.	W. Smith.	S. Smith.

H. WALKER, PRINTER, CLAY CROSS.

Whitwalk Festival, July 1884.

Grundy's Chapel, New Free Methodist, situated on Grundy Road, often referred to as Sugar Row, was opened by George Grundy for fellow workmen in December 1857. George was an iron moulder with the CXC. In 1910, it was converted into a bakehouse 'with an up to date oven' and has been used, until 1995, for a variety of business.

New Connexion Methodist Whitwalk dray, depicting, 'Wine is a Mocker and Deceiver', *c.* 1920. In 1903 bannerettes were awarded for the first time to the best turned out sunday schools in the procession. The best decorated 'cars' was another feature introduced at this time. Both were considered to be very successful additions to the traditional activities and became a permanent feature of the Whitwalks. The Primitive Methodists won the first prize in 1903.

The Spiritualist Church situated on Bridge Street. This was erected in 1935 by the Clay Cross Social Services Committee, 'That the work of this council be to alleviate the evils due to unemployment by providing a workshop, or workshops, and recreation centre and in such other ways as may lie in our power'. It was later designated as a Womens' Club and when the committee was disbanded, on the 16th December 1954, it was sold to the Salvation Army for £350.

Clay Cross Girls Friendly Society 1934, displaying the Diocesan Challenge Shield which they won for the fourth successive year. Back row, left to right: J. Elliot, A. Anthony, M. Hawkins, J. Jackson, C. Clark, M. Martin. Second row: E. Martin, E. Wheatcroft, Q. Butterworth, D. Fox, F. Allsop, D. Clegg, M. Jennison, P. Ghost. Seated: Q. Marshall, M. Wheatley, Mrs Ghost, Rev. S. Elder, Mrs Elwer. Kneeling: E. Lynham, J. Armstrong, R. Holmes, D. Butterworth, S. Marshall, E. Messenger.

The Whit Parade in 1963 on its way to Clay Cross Hall where the successive CXC managers resided and where their wives and daughters distributed the 'procession bun'. These processions to the Hall commenced in about 1862 and continued unbroken for many years. In 1875 the procession was described as, 'a very large one' and took twenty-five minutes to pass a certain point. The last walk from the Hall, with a much depleted following, was completed in 1993.

The Reorganised Church of the Latterday Saints situated on Revill Street, now renamed Broadleys, was built by Eustace Tinkler for the sum of £300. It was opened 28th April 1901, by J.W. Rushworth of Leeds. The major benefactor was Simon Holmes who joined the Church in 1877 and was ordained an elder in 1886. They first worshipped in the Angel Pub club-room and their first chapel was opened in a terraced row in New Street (King Stret).

Twelve

Streets and Buildings

Clay Cross High Street, *c.* 1920. Victoria Buidings, on the left, were built by Abraham Linacre in 1878 on the site of West Tunnel Row, which he purchased from the CXC in December 1876 for £1,813. Linacre had made a fortune in Melbourne, Austrailia and built much property in the town including his new residence, Melbourne Lodge, at the top of Springfields. On the right is East Tunnel Row, built in 1838 by the N.M.R. for their 'superior workmen', working on the tunnel. The CXC purchased both East and West Tunnel Rows in 1841, for £2,684. Property owned by the CXC was the only property in the town to be numbered for a considerable time, commencing with East Tunnel Row, 1 to 16 and West Tunnel Row, 17 to 30. East Tunnel Row was demolished in 1964.

Election time in Top Long Row. This photograph was taken during the 1922 Parliamentary Elections, with every house displaying a Charlie Duncan poster. The Top and Bottom Long Rows, with forty four houses in each row, were built between May and December 1840, and were the first workers houses to be built by George Stephenson. From December 1840 there is a reference to, 'John Furniss, to glazing 88 cottages at £1 8s 6d each'.

Cellar Row (twenty two houses), situated on the High Street, was also built by the CXC, c. 1845. In February 1910, the CXC decided to install four experimental water closets in this row and, if considered a success, 'and are not blocked periodically by all sorts of rubbish being put down them (as has been the case in the John Street property) more will be converted, as the opportunity offers'.

Pleasant Row (10 houses), was sometimes referred to as Gallows Row. It was situated opposite Cellar Row and was built by the CXC at about the same time, on top of the tunnel spoils. A substantial retaining wall was required to hold the spoils back. In Clay Cross at the begining of February 1910, there were only twelve slop water closets, twenty four ordinary water closets and no pail closets. The rest of the town had privy middens which were emptied infrequently.

Chapel Row (9 houses) was situated immediately above Pleasant Row and next to the New Connexion Methodists. Commenting on colliers housing, Rollinson, a Chesterfield architect, emphasised that, 'All pictorial effects must be dispensed with as unnecessary and misplaced, the object being to obtain models of utility and not ornament'.

Front view of Elbow Row (10 houses), were situated in Market Street and built in around.1848. Rollinson recommended that windows in colliers houses, 'should not be glazed in large squares in order to avoid a serious outlay in the case of breakage or if a partial breakage the substitution of putty or a paper patch'. It has been suggested that these buildings were originally built for stables and a reference for 6th June 1849, records, 'W.Babbs to have Stables House'.

A rear view of Elbow Row. These houses were built one up and one down with 'blind-backs'. The flimsy, single brick 'lean-to's' were not added on, by the CXC, until 1960 and were still rented out, until their final demolition in 1973. Through ventilation by incorporating back doors was not completed until 1915.

The Danesmoor Blocks celebrate the 1937 Coronation. Coinciding with the completion of the Parkhouse No.7 Pit in 1866, the company built fifty six new cottages at a cost of £5,451 and the improved aspect of these cottages was such that each block of eight houses had a communal washhouse and bakehouse, but no baths. Similar blocks were built by the company at Morton and Stonebroom for their No.5 and No.6 Pits.

Clay Lane Row (14 houses) was also built by the CXC c.1846. These were situated at the top of Clay Lane, just below the George and Dragon Pub and adjacent to the Old Stable School. Up to the end of 1848, the CXC had built some 208 workers' cottages and as their production was mainly for domestic coal, they relied on 'private' housing to accommodate extra workers during boom periods. Many workers were laid off during the summer periods when the demand for coal was low.

Above: Peter's Square, situated at the top of Holmgate and opposite Kennings Park entrance to the library. This row was built 'blind-back', by a speculator developer and during the 1850s it was mainly occupied by the Southern Irish, hence its name, after St Peter. According to the 1851 census these houses were severely overcrowded and in one house of two up and two down, there was a family of six with fourteen lodgers – and no shift work!

Left: Dore's Yard, or Irish Yard, situated next to Peter's Square, was also built 'blind-back' and until the time they were demolished, they never had running water. Water was collected from a stand pipe situated in the middle of the row. The first house in this row, from about 1894, was a general stores shop set up by Mr Jack Renshaw, after he had been locked out and victimised by the company.

Chapel Street, c. 1974, was situated at the top of Holmgate, next to the Post Office. This row was built c.1848 by Robert Hazeldine and the 1851 census referred to Hazeldine's Row. Hazeldine was the landlord of the Blue Bell Inn which was next to the Toll House on the High Street, purchased by Mr J. Unwin in September 1871. He demolished it and built the premises that now houses the Post Office.

Stoppards' Row, Market Street, c. 1960. This row was built and owned by the Stoppard family, an old Clay Cross yeoman and blacksmithing family. Mary Stoppard, born in 1842, died in Stoppards' Row in April 1935 at the age of 93. The 1861 census records the CXC's first colliery hospital situated at the end of this row. It was occupied by Isaac Kenning, coal miner, Mary his wife, nurse and William Elliot, a patient, aged 15.

Above: Waterloo Street taken from the Goods Yard, *c.* 1968. This Goods Yard was opened up in January 1885. 'Some inconvieniance having been felt by trades people, owners and residents in the town of Clay Cross through the non-existance of a central railway goods depot – the result is that a commodious goods shed at the terminus of Clay Cross branch line, which is near the Market Place, has been secured and arrangements have been made by which goods can be brought and taken to the station or mainline over a mile distant.

Left: Waterloo Street with Park Row at the bottom to the left. There were two rows in Waterloo Street which were known as the 'Monkey Hollow' and were built around the late 50s early 60's and at one time owned by Stephen Bircumshaw. They were amongst the most neglected property in the town and in September 1877, the owners and occupiers were served notice by the L.B.H to limewash, or otherwise clean, their houses.

Tupton Hall, c. 1920. This hall was built in 1650, by the Gladwin family who came to reside at Tupton about 1634. In 1839 it was rented from Anne Lord by George Stephenson and Company to accommodate Charles Binns the company's agent until 1845. Anne Lord married Fredrick Packman MD and they returned to Tupton Hall after Binns moved to Clay Cross. With the demise of Anne Packman in 1889, it was leased out by their daughter to Arthur G.Barnes.

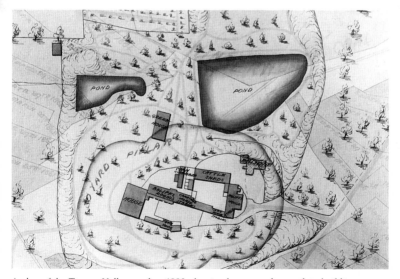

A plan of the Tupton Hall grounds, c.1880, showing house, gardens and outbuildings. The Hall and estate were purchased by the Derbyshire County Council in 1929 and plans approved for a Secondary School in 1935. The School was opened Thursday 8th October 1936, by Mr Oliver Stanley MP. It was gutted by fire on Saturday 2nd July, 1938, destroying a famous Adam ceiling that incorporated the Gladwin Coat of Arms.

Clay Cross Hall was built for Charles Binns in 1845 and used rent free together with free coal and a cow. It cost £625 to build. 'There is in course of erection a large mansion intended for the residence of the manager, the site which is well chosen in a picturesque country adjacent to the works, it is a first rate building, ornamented with rich stone work, combining comfort with decoration suitable for the residence of a gentleman'. It was sold to the County Council for £4,000 in November 1949.

Office House, situated at the bottom of Eldon Street, was completed in February 1840 and is one of the few remaining structures built by Stephenson. The first person to reside there was Henry Wilkinson, the company's cashier who died prematurely in 1842. It was later converted into two cottages for the Company's middle management. The house to the left was Rose Cottage and the other Eldon House. The windows for this house were glazed for £1 8s in December 1840 by John Furniss.

Above: Hill House was built by Abraham Gent in 1833 and sold to the N.M.R in February 1837. It was then used as an office by Fredrick Swanwick, resident engineer, during the tunnelling operations. It was purchased by the CXC in 1840 for £630 and then occupied by James Campbell, the company engineer until 1846. William Howe, engineer, followed and he was replaced by Binn's son-in-law, Dr Wilson, company surgeon who occupied the house until 1866.

Right: An advert for the sale of Hill House February 1837. The Gent family came to this farm at Danesmoor in about 1720 and Abraham Gent Jnr was the first known estate agent in the parish and recieved an Appraisers License in June 1803. He was buried in North Wingfield Church Yard on the 24th April 1836, aged 61 years. Gents Hill at Danesmoor was named after this family and small colliery was sunk here in about the mid 1850s.

Springfield House was built in 1866 for William Howe at a cost of £626. The managers' houses were just as 'tied' as those of the workers and when their employment ceased the houses were vacated, irrespective of loyalty, allegiance and length of service. Charles Binns accrued forty seven years service as manager but when he died in January 1887, his widow had to vacate the house by March. All the household furniture and effects were sold off by auction.

Gaffer's Row or Egstow Terrace, was purpose built for the compny's middle managers in 1846 at a cost of £574 or £143 each. This row was more substantial than any of the workers' cottages with four rooms up and four rooms down and extensive cellars. The 1851 census recorded the following residents in this small but exclusive row: Benjamin Turner, agent; John Hudson, company school teacher; Thomas Martin, deputy and John Parker, colliery agent.

Whitworth's Row once situated on Broadley's. This row appears to have been built during the 1860s and named after William Whitworth who was a blacksmith and landlord of the Blacksmith Arms (now the Three Horse Shoes). The first reference to him with regards selling beer is in 1849, and refers to House, Parlour and Club-room. In the 1851 census he is recorded as a publican and smith. He died in 1871, and was still landlord of the Three Horse Shoes. Broadleys was not adopted as a Public Highway until October 1903

The Kings Head on Thanet Street showing the end of Cross Street. In the 1841 and 1851 census Samuel Hays is recorded as a Publican (no pub name). In 1860 Mrs Hays is recorded as the landlady of the Kings Head and the following year her son William was landlord and in January 1862 the Chesterfield Brewery had purchased the pub. Henry Farnsworth was landlord in 1871 and in 1881 it was Thomas Holland, until 1908.

Victoria's Diamond Jubilee parade in June 1897. This procession commenced in the schoolyard at 12.30 p.m. and was headed by the Tibshelf Brass Band and followed by the Sunday School scholars, U.D.C. Fire Brigade and the Friendly Societies. The line of the route was decorated with bunting and flags. A large bonfire was lighted at 10pm on the No.1 Pit tip at a fair-ground. All those people in receipt of parish relief were treated to a knife-and-fork tea and the men were given a pipe of tobacco and the women two ounces of tea.